THINGS MY MAMA SAID

WRITTEN BY

JUDY BARKER AUSTIN

All rights reserved. No part of this book may be reproduced in any form or by any means, without permission of HIGH ROAD LLC.

First Edition, April 2016

ISBN-13:978-0692696910

ISBN-10:0692696911

BIASC: Self-Help/Motivational & Inspirational

Judy Barker Austin
P. O. Box 94
Centerville, IA 52544

Email: judybarkeraustin.highroad@gmail.com

The year 1936 was full of events . . .
- The Hoover Dam was completed;
- Margaret Mitchell's *Gone with the Wind* was first published;
- Joe Louis got knocked out in the 12th round at Yankee Stadium;
- President Franklin Delano Roosevelt was re-elected;
- Jesse Owens won 4 Gold Medals at the Summer Olympics in Berlin, Germany;
- Actors Robert Redford, Alan Alda, Michael Landon, Burt Reynolds, and Mary Tyler Moore--Singers Glen Campbell and Roy Orbison--and Senator and War Hero John McCain were all born;
- And Russian Psychologist Ivan Pavlov--Writer Rudyard Kipling--and Monarch George V died.

Yet with all these important events, the 1936 event that impacted my life the most was that my **Mama was born.**

ACKNOWLEDGEMENT

I credit my daughter Jenny Austin for inspiring me to write this book.

Four years ago Jenny and I were in Hannibal, Missouri, for a mother/daughter Mother's Day weekend. She bought me a small writer's book at the Mark Twain Museum for me to use to jot down inspirational ideas and experiences.

On the drive back home to Centerville, Iowa, I told her about how Mama (her Grandma Barker) had a lot of witty sayings and how they had helped to guide me throughout my life. Jenny said, "You should write a book about those sayings and call it Things My Mama Said."

She picked up the book she had given me and asked what some of the sayings were. I started calling them out, and she wrote them down in the book. Thank you, Jenny, for one of the best Mother's Day I have ever had. I really enjoyed our weekend in Hannibal. Also, thanks for your ideas that encouraged me to write this memorial to Mama.

I also want to acknowledge my daughter Katie Austin for helping me edit the book. You were truly a lifesaver. You resemble Mama so much when she was young. I feel her spirit whenever I am around you.

Thanks to my brother Ros Barker for his contributions to the book as well as his help in editing. You have such a creative mind. Keep writing.

My son Stephen Austin has always been the biggest supporter of my writing. He has read every word of all my books and always has excellent commentary. Don't give up on your dreams, Stephen.

Thanks, also, to my cousins Gladys Hardin Barker and Wilma Faye (Tootsie) Barker Humphres for their insight into the time Mama went on her adventure to California. Thank you so much, Tootsie, for taking care of me and my brother Ronald when Mama was "California Dreaming."

Mama and Daddy, Summer 1960.

TABLE OF CONTENTS

CHAPTER ONE – HELLO--LET ME INTRODUCE YOU TO MAMA.

CHAPTER TWO – CHILDREN ARE A GIFT FROM GOD. (Practice Philoteknos)

CHAPTER THREE – GIVE THINGS A LITTLE TIME AND THEN SEE HOW YOU FEEL. (Consider Giving Second Chances)

CHAPTER FOUR – VOTE FOR THE CUTEST ONE. (Have a Sense of Humor)

CHAPTER FIVE – IT'S NEVER WHOM YOU EXPECT. (Anticipate the Unexpected)

CHAPTER SIX – REGARDLESS OF WHAT YOU BELIEVE, I'M FROM VINA. (Know Who You Are and What You Stand For)

CHAPTER SEVEN – YOU GOT SOME FUZZ IN THERE AMONGST ALL THAT OTHER FUZZ. (Help Others)

CHAPTER EIGHT – I'LL SEE YOU WHEN I SEE YOU. (Accept and Love Family Unconditionally)

CHAPTER NINE – DO YOU WANT TO TALK TO YOUR DADDY? (Show Respect)

CHAPTER TEN – LET'S MAKE SLAW. (Nurture Relationships)

CHAPTER ELEVEN – I'LL LIVE UNTIL I DIE. (Be Thankful)*

*This book is based on my recollections of the memories, experiences, and events that are important to me about Mama. I realize other individuals who knew her have their own memories and perceptions of her, which may be very different from mine.

Random Pictures of Mama. She Always Smiled for the Camera.

Some mothers are kissing mothers and some are scolding mothers, but it is love just the same, and most mothers kiss and scold together. ~~~Pearl S. Buck

CHAPTER ONE – HELLO--LET ME INTRODUCE YOU TO MAMA.

Tamara Marie Furman was born to Joseph Adam Furman and Helen Marie Navoiczyk Furman in Kenosha, Wisconsin, on the 128th day of the year 1936 of the Gregorian Calendar (May 7). Back then Kenosha was the home of Nash Motors Company, known for inventing heating and seatbelts in cars.

She applied for her first job at 16 and had to secure a copy of her birth certificate. That's when she found out her birth month (May) was listed as her middle name on the legal document instead of Marie. When she asked why she had never been informed of this mistake, her mother in a thick Belarussian/Polish accent declared, "Marie I name you, and Marie you are." Mama reluctantly gave up thinking of herself as Tamara Marie and used Tamara May the rest of her life which heightened her annoyance with her mom and set up yet one more of many barriers they had between them.

Mama's Dad (whom she called Pa) passed away when she was only 12 years old. She told me once how things had changed so horribly for her when her Pa died. Mama felt Pa had loved her the most, and her mother loved her brother Leon the most. After her Pa died, she felt there was no one to love her and care about her.

I once asked Mama why she never bought cut flowers or enjoyed getting flower arrangements. She said every time she smelled cut flowers their sickeningly, sweet aroma made her nauseous, and the smell transported her back in time to her Pa's funeral where she saw his casket surrounded by so many flowers. Mama idolized him, and he had been her protector from the harsh and constant criticisms of her mother. She suspected her mom had been jealous of their close relationship. I think Mama was correct as she was soon whisked off to a Catholic boarding school 40 miles away and had little contact with her mother for the next four years.

Mama was extremely intelligent (but stubborn) and graduated from the boarding school only a few days after her 16th birthday. She would have finished over 6 months earlier, but was held there until she finished sewing what she referred to as "that ugly jumper." Mama thought it was ridiculous that sewing an article of clothing was a requirement to graduate from high school. Therefore, she refused to even start to stitch it for several months. The nuns stood firm and wouldn't let the school issue her a diploma until the jumper was sewn to their liking. When she finally acknowledged they were more stubborn than she, Mama completed the jumper and received her diploma. She told me as soon as the diploma was in her hand, the jumper was in the trash never for her to view again.

She escaped the nuns to move back in with her estranged mother but never foresaw she would be jumping from the fire into enraging flames. Living with her mother for that next year, in Mama's own words was "pure hell." I loved both Mama and my

Grandma Furman and understood many of the reasons they didn't get along.

I believe Grandma was a perfectionist and expected her daughter to be perfect. Grandma was immaculate and tidy. Mama could care less if the floor had been swept or mopped or when the end tables had last been dusted. Grandma even brought her own toilet paper when she came for a visit.

Mama cooked, washed dishes, made her bed, and kept clothes clean and folded, but I never saw her do any yard work. As long as I lived at home, I never remember seeing her dust, and she rarely cared about how the inside of the house looked. On the other hand, Grandma Furman was always cleaning. Grandma came to visit one summer when I was in the 8th grade. Mama and I cleaned every possible minute for a week to have the house looking perfect. The first thing Grandma did after putting down her suitcases in my room was to drop down on her hands and knees and peer under my bed. She found a small dust bunny under there, much to my chagrin. Grandma immediately pulled a tissue from her purse, scooped up the dust ball, and trotted me to the garbage can to dispose of it as she gave me a 10 minute lecture on how cleanliness was important everywhere--even under the bed.

Mama was able to break away from her mother's constant criticism during the daylight hours as she quickly secured a job in Racine, 11 miles from Kenosha. She walked quite a distance to a bus stop to board a bus that took her to and from work each day. A couple of weeks after her 17th birthday close to that same bus stop is where she met Daddy. (You might be interested to know this was the same street her mother had met her dad. Before you ask, I must tell you I never wandered up and down that street searching for me a husband, although I have contemplated the action several times.)

Daddy, at the tender age of 21, had traveled up from impoverished Alabama along with several of his same-age nephews to secure jobs. They were cruising along when they zeroed in on an attractive, young woman walking down the street. They immediately pulled over and asked if she needed a lift; without hesitation she jumped in the car with them. A couple of Daddy's nephews thought Mama would be a perfect match for them, but she only had eyes for Pete Barker.

Pete Barker was 6'6" with dark, wavy hair, and brilliant blue eyes. Mama said she was immediately attracted to his height as she was 5'9" and usually towered above the boys she met who were interested in her. But, by far, her biggest attraction to Daddy was his curly hair.

Mama was obsessed with curly hair. I distinctly recall seeing her down on her knees praying to God her daughter would have curly hair. That's the only thing I recall her openly praying to God about.

God never answered those prayers. She decided I would have curly hair whether God ordained it or not. She began giving me cheap home perms that burned my scalp and made me look like I had a huge dark Brillo pad on top of my head. When she couldn't afford the perm kits, she twisted my wet hair into what seemed like hundreds of tiny balls and flattened them onto my head with two bobby pins per ball making an X that I had to sleep on at night to give me a temporary look of curls. I endured this torture until the summer before the 8th grade when I had a growth spurt that ended with my being able to look her eye to eye and declare I was never going to have curly hair and would never let her put a perm or bobby pin in my hair again. (I still cringe when I see a bobby pin lying around.)

I was an adult before I learned Daddy was first attracted to Mama because of the noticeable gap between her front teeth and she to his thick, curly hair. Ironically, Daddy lost most of his hair in his early 30s, and Mama lost the gap between her teeth in her late 20s. She had to have all her teeth pulled and had false teeth from that point forward.

From the beginning of their relationship, Mama refused to call Daddy by his nickname, Pete. His name was actually Ros Buford Barker. At first, she called him Ros, then later Buford. Growing up, I only heard her refer to him as "Your Daddy."

Daddy went back to Alabama only a few weeks after they met. (This behavior remained a pattern for the first 9 years of my life. Daddy would search for work, only to find none. Then we would travel up to either Kenosha, Wisconsin, or Zion, Illinois, where he would find a job and make a little money.

He would then get homesick for Alabama, and we would head back south where he once again would be unable to find work.)

He soon placed a phone call to Mama to ask if she wanted to come down to Alabama. She said, "Sure, but you have to come get me and take me down there." She already had plans to go to the beach with some of her friends after work on the day he said he would pick her up. Mama didn't know for sure if Daddy would show up or why he had invited her to Alabama. Daddy was a man of few words and hadn't revealed if he wanted her to come for a visit or to marry him. Being the optimist she always was, she put on her bathing suit, pulled on a dress on top of it, packed a bag with a few clothes and personal items, and waited. If he arrived on time, she would go to Alabama with him. If not, she would proceed with her previous plans and go swimming in Lake Michigan with her friends.

When she heard the honk of Daddy's car horn, she hurried outside and down the steps tightly clutching her bag. Grandma Furman was right behind her waving her arms demanding to know where her daughter was going. Daddy did not get out of the car. He had always refused to get out of the car and come inside to meet Grandma, and he hadn't planned to make any changes on that day. Mama never acknowledged Grandma's presence as she threw her bag in the back seat through the rolled down window and opened the front passenger door to leap in the front seat. Grandma's fingers literally grazed the door handle as Mama jerked the car door shut and the car lurched forward. Mama was heading south on an adventure with the man of her dreams. She looked straight ahead and definitely not in the rearview mirror, where she would have seen Grandma standing by the curb with hands on her hips and fire in her eyes.

A Justice of the Peace married them on Friday, July 3, 1953, in Fulton, Mississippi. Mama still wore her bathing suit beneath her dress. Why Fulton? Mississippi law allowed a woman to get married at 17 where in Alabama she had to be 18. Mama and Daddy had only known each other for five weeks.

Mama and Daddy a Few Months After They Married. She Was Already Pregnant With Me.

I was born 10 ½ months after they married and 11 days after Mama's 18th birthday.

Mama had never been around children and often told me she had no idea of how to be a mother. Mama also shared she felt she had "practiced" on me. We were more like friends than mother and daughter. She treated me like a small adult--never a child.

When I was in my late 20s, my cousin R. C. Humphres told me Mama taught me to play Rummy and Black Jack when I was only 2 years old so she would have someone to play cards with. He said I was so small I could barely hold all the Rummy cards at once--even using both hands. I guess my love of card playing is something I owe to Mama.

She taught me to read before I was 3 and instilled in me my love for reading. I don't think I ever saw Mama sit down without a book close by. I think she may have had a photographic memory, or very close to it, as she seemed to remember everything she read and knew the correct answer to any question I ever asked her.

Mama's birthday was always close to Mother's Day. I wrote this book about Mama to commemorate what would have been her 80th birthday. This special birthday is May 7, 2016, just a few days after this book is available for the public. I also am using it to say Happy Mother's Day.

A mother is one to whom you hurry to when you are troubled. ~~~Emily Dickinson

So Happy 80th Birthday, and Happy Mother's Day, Mama. I love you and appreciate all the wisdom and love you gave me.

I also wrote this book to share with you some of Mama's wit and wisdom. It's a celebration of her life, and I hope you can use some of her unique sayings to laugh, cry, and maybe even become a better person.

I am honored to share some of her life with you. She was a rare person who never received the accolades she so richly deserved.

* * *

Mama, 8 Years Old With Leon, Her Brother.

One of Mama's School Pictures.

Mama With Her Parents and Brother Leon; Mama Showing Off That Famous Gap Between Her Teeth; Mama and Uncle Leon; Mama in Braids; and Mama With Grandma Furman When Mama Was a Baby.

CHAPTER TWO – CHILDREN ARE A GIFT FROM GOD. (Practice Philoteknos)

"Dearest Judy,

You know talking about a past, I'd rather forget, has really given me a lot to think about. Where do adults get the idea they can impose their will on children without considering them as human beings, saying the most terrible things to them? I don't know what they are thinking about, or if they think about it at all. All people were children at one time, and it really wasn't that long ago.

Do people become what they are because of their parents or in spite of them? It bears thinking about. You really are taking on a heavy responsibility. While children are young, you think you have all the time in the world, but it's all a lie, and we are only given our children as a gift from God for a very brief season and really should do the best we can for them while we can. Boy, isn't that HEAVY?

Well, since I've cheered you up, I'll close for now and trot this letter down to the Post Office.

Love you,
Your Mama"

The excerpt on the previous page is from a letter I found in a box filled with old pictures back in the summer of 2013. It was dated February 21, 1984, two and a half months before my first child was born. I think what inspired Mama to write this letter was the conversation we had had a few days prior about her childhood and the volatile love/hate relationship she had with her own mom.

Mama believed children were a gift from God. Do you believe that as well? Or do you believe your children are only here to fulfill your unfulfilled dreams and aspirations?

Ayelet Waldman, the author of the book *Bad Mother*, points out how the most toxic thing parents can do is allow delight and pride in their children to be spoiled because the children couldn't live up to preconceived parental expectations. Many expectations were in place before the children were born--securing their failure. Those expectations have nothing to do with the children but everything to do with the parents' own egos.

What would you give up for your child? Your own life? Money?

Cheryl Anderson was an ordinary person who did something quite extraordinary. She wasn't someone I have ever heard of or have ever met. Yet when I read about her story online, I could not hold back my tears.

When she was 2 months pregnant and only 32 years old, she went to the doctor because of a small lump on her neck. The biopsy showed it was cancer. Chemotherapy would give her a chance to live but harm her baby. She decided she would refuse the chemotherapy and give up her life for her unborn daughter. Without chemotherapy to stop the spread of cancer, it continued to grow. Cheryl consented to radiotherapy because it would extend her life without harming the baby. Cheryl fought hard to take her pregnancy to 6 months. She then became so weak her doctor had to conduct an emergency caesarean section. When she woke up from the surgery, she was told her daughter Taylor had survived and was doing well. Cheryl drifted away and died a few hours later.

Adam LaRoche, baseball player for the Chicago White Sox, gave up $13 million for his 14-year-old son. Adam had 6 months left on his contract and would get $13 million but quit the White Sox team when told his son Drake would not be allowed to hang around the clubhouse any longer. LaRoche said he had no regrets, and there was more to life than baseball. I'm sure this was not an easy thing to do, especially for a man whose brother and father had also played pro baseball.

You don't have to give up your job or your life for your child, but you can work on having a good relationship.

Jennifer Lopez is an incredibly busy lady. She acts, sings, and dances. I read an article about her at a time when she was an American Idol judge, the leading character on a TV series, had just come out with a new movie and music CD, and was finishing up the choreography and song list for her new Las Vegas show. In the article, Jennifer shared how important is was for her to nurture her relationship with her children. She said her children knew Mommy is busy, but they also knew they were her stars.

What is your relationship with your child or children like? Is it weak? Broken? Studies in bonding and attachment prove children must have sustained and stable physical and emotional contact with their parent or parents.

Below are some guidelines to help in repairing a weak and/or broken relationship with your child or children.

1. REACH OUT.

Nothing can happen unless someone takes the initiative to reach out. In fact, it may take several attempts before you triumph in even commencing successful communication.

2. BE AVAILABLE.

What good is it to reach out and then not be available? Be willing to set aside time for frank discussions and possible reconciliation.

3. USE CONFLICT RESOLUTION SKILLS.

In my *Always Take the High Road* book, I mention how there are **5 A's of Conflict Resolution.**

1) **A**cknowledge the Conflict - When you acknowledge there is a conflict, it is the first step to solving a conflict.

2) **A**nalyze the Conflict - You have to decide if the conflict is something you can control or can't control.

3) **A**ssess your Contribution to the Conflict – Ask the question, "What part did I play in the conflict?

4) **A**lter Perceptions – Seek to understand the other person's point of view, and don't have a victim mentality.

5) Take **A**ction – After accomplishing the first 4 **A's,** you should do something while having the goal to resolve and repair the conflict--not fan the flames.

4. DON'T BE AFRAID TO SAY, "I'M SORRY."

It takes a strong and confident person to admit to being wrong. When you recognize and admit your faults, it's easier for your children to admit their faults. Then the healing process can begin.

5. STAY IN TOUCH.

Once the relationship has started to heal, it will take nurturing. With today's extensive list of ways to communicate, there's no excuse for not keeping the lines of communication open.

The above guidelines can also be applied to a situation where you are the child interested in repairing a relationship with your parent or parents. Alan Loy McGinnis's book, *Confidence: How to Succeed at Being Yourself,* has a list of 12 Rules for Building Self-Confidence. Number 8 on the list says you should make the best possible peace with your parents.

Children are a heritage from the LORD, offspring a reward from him. ~~~Psalms 127:3

The Greek word "philoteknos" represents a very special kind of love called "mother love." It stems from the belief that as mothers love and care for their children, those actions result in the understanding of how children are a unique gift from God.

Mothers should love and care for their children; however, the ability to love and care for a child may have to be taught. In the 2nd Chapter of Titus, Apostle Paul instructs women who were older in their knowledge of the Gospel to teach the younger women to love their children.

Dorothy can attest to this as her mother paid little attention to her. When her parents divorced,

Dorothy's mom sent 8-year-old Dorothy and younger sister Isabelle on an unsupervised train ride from Illinois to California to live with harsh and unloving paternal grandparents. Because of her abusive circumstances, Dorothy left her grandparents at age 14 during the Great Depression and soon found work as a housekeeper and nanny. Her employer and a couple of teachers became the mother Dorothy never had. She was encouraged to read, go to school, and graduate from high school. Dorothy traveled back to Illinois after graduating with the hope of reuniting with a mother who loved and wanted her. Unfortunately, her mother did not, which once again left Dorothy alone with nowhere to go.

Years later when Dorothy had her own daughter, she was determined to be the mother her mother had not been. She was successful as her daughter, Hillary Rodham Clinton, often remarked no one had a bigger influence on her life or did more to shape who she was than her mother.

Dorothy's trials and tribulations impacted Hillary who has fought and continues to fight to protect children's rights.

If we were not fortunate to have a good mother, we can break the pattern and become a good mother to our daughters and sons.

Mirror, mirror on the wall, I am my mother after all. ~~~Author Unknown

Grandma Furman was a wonderful grandmother to me, and I knew she loved me. Unfortunately, Mama never perceived her to be a good mother to her. I facilitated a complete reconciliation between Mama and Grandma only a couple of years before Grandma died. I consider this one of my greatest accomplishments in life as I dearly loved them both. Below is a picture of my Grandma Furman, Helen Navoiczyk Furman.

* * *

A grandmother is a little bit parent, a little bit teacher, and a little bit best friend.
~~~Anonymous

WHAT I CAN DO TO BE A BETTER PARENT OR BETTER CHILD.

_____

_____

_____

_____

_____

CHAPTER THREE – GIVE THINGS A LITTLE TIME AND THEN SEE HOW YOU FEEL. (Consider Giving Second Chances)

Mama was all about second chances.

When I was four and living in Kenosha, Mama left me, my brother Ronald, and Daddy to go cash a check for a relative. She cashed the check and bought a bus ticket to where she felt was as far away from Kenosha as she could get--Los Angeles, California. Mama found a room at the YWCA and was soon hired as a statistical typist.

She was 22 with a 4-year-old and a 1 ½-year-old. She felt her 26-year old husband didn't appreciate her and was taking advantage of her. Daddy was #14 out of 15 kids, so his nephews and nieces were closer to his age than his older brothers and sisters. He always seemed to have a bevy of relatives and friends hanging around expecting Mama to continually wait on them and do their bidding.

For years, I wondered why Mama came back. When I asked her why, she confessed she had a good life in Los Angeles and could have easily supported herself in a job she loved but missed her children and husband. Mama thought Daddy deserved a second chance even though he hadn't treated her well. I know my brothers Ros and John are glad she returned since they weren't even born yet.

Gabby, a former student of mine, went through a lot of heartaches and tribulations with her ex-husband.

Then the day came when she decided to give him a second chance. He had suffered a stroke which almost killed him. This was most unfortunate as he had decided to become a better person which resulted in his being sober for nearly two years. His brain surgeon called his survival a miracle and that he had defeated death.

Gabby made a brave and selfless decision to help him in his recovery. Since they were no longer married, this was not something she was obligated to do.

With her help, encouragement, and prayers, he continued to recover and started walking and talking again.

I was impressed by her enthusiasm when she told me he reached the stage in his physical therapy where he was able to walk over 600 steps a day and was now "walking all over the house."

Even though there are days that often wear her out, she says praying for someone and taking care of them is what you do for someone you love. Gabby dismissed the sacrifice she made for him by saying, "We've been through a lot worse."

Second chances don't always mean a happy ending. Sometimes it's just another shot to end things right.

Here are 8 things to contemplate when considering giving someone a second chance.

1. KNOW WHEN ENOUGH IS ENOUGH.

Giving someone a second chance can be compared to giving a shooter another bullet after they missed you the first time. Before you know it that one chance bullet has turned into two bullets and then it's two too many--and you're caught in a *"bob n' weave"* dance.

Yet sometimes enough is not enough, especially if they deserve the second chance, and you have it within you to grant that second chance.

2. DECIDE AND CONCENTRATE ON WHAT PART OF THE SECOND CHANCE WILL WORK.

As I wrote in my *Always Take The High Road* book, attempt only what you have at least an 80% chance of accomplishing. Why give someone a second chance at something you know in your "heart of hearts" is not attainable? Also, realize it may need to result in compromise. You may not be able to get it all your way.

3. DO YOUR HOMEWORK.

Should you even be considering the person as someone who deserves a second chance? If the individual is, what about the deed that was done? If it is too serious, he or she may not deserve a second chance. Research and consider all the facts related to the issue. This means you have to be honest with yourself on how you contributed to the issue(s).

4. GIVE YOURSELF SOME TIME.

You don't want to give the second chance too soon, nor do you want to deny it before you have given yourself the appropriate amount of time to consider all options. Mama didn't go to California for only a week or two. She was there for several months. She gave herself the time needed to make her decision to give Daddy a second chance.

5. FOLLOW YOUR INSTINCTS.

In his book, *The Gift of Fear,* Gavin de Becker, discusses how within each of us we have innate survival signals to help protect us from harm. He specifically discusses how people who are trying to deceive tend to give too many details. They do this because they fear they will be doubted. My friend Martha Ann has told me many times, "When someone shows you who he is--believe him." Second chances can be good; it's just some people don't deserve them.

6. INVOLVE AS FEW UNINVOLVED PEOPLE AS POSSIBLE.

It's always useful to have a good friend or close family member to confide in, but don't tell everyone about your situation. Mama didn't go around telling everyone why she went out to California or why she came back. She didn't talk about Daddy to other people. She knew to involve as few uninvolved people as possible.

7. LEARN FROM YOUR MISTAKES.

I saw a quote once that said, *"Sometimes second chances work out even better than the first because you learn from your mistakes."* The question may then become, "Can you learn from your mistakes?" What has your track record been? Do you usually learn from mistakes, or do you keep making the same mistakes over and over while learning nothing?

8. DON'T WASTE THE SECOND CHANCE IF IT'S BEEN GIVEN TO YOU.

It could be the best gift anyone's ever given you. It could change your life for good. It could add value to your self-esteem. Appreciate the second chance, and don't take it for granted.

An eye for an eye and the whole world goes blind. ~~~ Gandhi

Nelle Wilson Reagan, the mother of President Ronald Reagan, was a believer in giving second chances. She visited jails and read the Bible to inmates. When they were released from prison, she allowed them to stay their first night of freedom in the Reagan home. If you've ever wondered where President Reagan got his moral principles and perpetual optimism, now you know. It was from his mother, Nelle.

**Mama, Ronald, and Me
Shortly Before She Left
For California.**

* * *

WHAT I CAN DO TO GIVE THINGS A LITTLE TIME AND THEN SEE HOW I FEEL.

_____

_____

_____

_____

_____

God could not be everywhere. So he created mothers. ~~~Jewish Proverb

CHAPTER FOUR – VOTE FOR THE CUTEST ONE. (Have a Sense of Humor)

As a kid, I remember Mama telling me joke after joke. Lots of knock, knock jokes. Even though they weren't always politically correct or funny, she told me little moron jokes and Polish jokes. Maybe she rationalized the Polish jokes were ok since her Pa had immigrated from Poland and she was half Polish.

Some of the ones I remember are:

Question: Why did the little moron throw the clock out the window? Answer: He wanted to see time fly.

Knock, Knock. Who's there? Dewayne. Dewayne who? Dewayne the bathtub; I'm dwowning!

Question: Why don't Pollocks have ice cubes? Answer: They keep forgetting the recipe for them.

Question: What did the jar of mayonnaise say to the refrigerator? Answer: Close the door; I'm dressing.

We read Dr. Seuss books together and to my little brother Ronald. When we read the book, *Green Eggs and Ham*, I thought it was the silliest book I had ever read and told her so. "Judy, she said, sometimes silly is good. It can help you to laugh and get through those bad times."

I was aware there was a presidential election going on when I attended first grade in Zion, Illinois. I asked Mama who she was going to vote for. She laughed and said, "I'm voting for the cutest one." Well, I definitely didn't think Richard Nixon was cute so I assumed she was voting for John F. Kennedy. I knew Mama was making a joke of the question I asked. What I enjoyed was how she smiled and laughed at her own answer. I liked that she had a sense of humor.

A sense of humor is part of the art of leadership, of getting along with people, of getting things done. ~~~President Dwight Eisenhower

Last year I experienced one of those bad times Mama had warned me about. I turned on my TV to watch monkeys dancing on stage with Chris Martin (lead singer of the group Coldplay) and listened to the seemingly worthless lyrics of Ooh-ooh, ooh-ooh.

I picked up the remote to change the channel, but Mama's words came back to me. I put the remote down and allowed my worries and depression to slither away as I smiled and laughed at how silly Chris Martin looked. At that moment, I had an even deeper appreciation for Mama as well as those entertainers who make us smile and help us escape the tragedies and disappointments of our lives--at least for a few minutes.

So I totally relaxed and continued to enjoy the silliness of Chris Martin jumping up and down, pumping his arm in the air surrounded by his monkey companions as hundreds of multi-colored balloons cascaded onto the stage.

Mommies are just big little girls.
~~~Author Unknown

Because of Mama's lessons on silliness, I developed a keen sense of humor that has helped me through bad times and continues to help me through bad times.

Having a good sense of humor can help you on your job. An international survey found 91% of executives feel a good sense of humor can advance employees' careers. Eighty four percent of the same executives believed employees were more valuable if they possessed a good sense of humor.

Thanks to Mama I have eluded and improved numerous stressful work situations through using my sense of humor.

* * *

WHAT I CAN DO TO DEVELOP A GOOD SENSE OF HUMOR.

_____

_____

_____

_____

_____

CHAPTER FIVE – IT'S NEVER WHOM YOU EXPECT. (Anticipate the Unexpected)

Mama loved to watch the TV show, Perry Mason. I would watch it with her and within 5 minutes she would announce who the murderer was. She was always right. I remember one time I asked her how she could always be right. She told me, "It's never whom you expect."

Over fifty years later I was watching a Perry Mason marathon on the Hallmark station during Mama's birthday week. It seemed like a tribute to her and her murder case-solving skills. One episode consisted of a businessman who tries to cover for his felon friend while an extortionist gets murdered on his boat. I decided this was the perfect episode to test Mama's theory. I deduced the person I would least expect to be the murderer was the businessman's closest friend who did most of his work for him and regularly covered for him if he got into trouble. It wouldn't be the felon friend (who turns out to be his brother), his business partner, or his daughter (who turns out to be his brother's daughter and not his). It would have to be his loyal friend, and I was right.

Is Mama's phrase, "It's Never Whom You Expect," applicable to our lives today? If so, how? I think it means you have to keep your eyes open and know the times you should make decisions based on your "head" and not your "heart." There will be times when those you least expect can say and do things that throw you a curve ball. It could be a family member or a close friend.

A few years ago, I was severely depressed about not having a job or being able to find one. After applying for over 50 jobs with no success, I shared on Facebook how I would like for my friends and family to pray for me in finding a job. I also shared how if I couldn't find one, I might have to move.

A good friend saw the post and asked if I would be interested in a position that might soon be available in her business. It was an office job paying well below what I was accustomed to, but I thought I would, at least, hear her out because it could be mutually beneficial. A couple of days later I received a private Facebook message inquiring if I would come to her business for an "interview." I thought it was strange for her to call it an interview, but I said yes, printed up a couple copies of my resume, and drove over to see her. When I got there, she whisked me to the furthest point from the reception area to a most uncomfortable place to have an interview. She didn't ask me any questions. She proceeded to tell me how overqualified I was and how she and her husband had talked about how I wouldn't work out for them. I was not allowed to respond until the very end where I assured her if I were offered the position I would be a valuable asset to their organization. I left humiliated and beaten down. It's never a compliment to be told you are overqualified for a job when you really need one for your survival. Especially by a friend. I had not seen it coming from my friend. To my surprise, a week later I got a (what I felt was very condescending) rejection letter from her husband making me feel even worse as it recited all the reasons why I would not be a good fit for their business. At a time when I was very fragile, I had not expected my friends to assist in making me even more so. Another rejection and rejection letter was not what I needed and was by someone of whom was least expected.

When you are hit with the unexpected, you have to realize you can only control how you react to the situation. You cannot control the other person. I had to let my feelings go and not harbor resentment. I also tried to put everything in perspective and believe my friend actually thought she wanted to help me and probably didn't realize how her actions had hurt me.

This has been one of the harder lessons from Mama for me to learn. Maybe it's because I seem always to look for the best in people and situations.

Here are some ways to help when dealing with the unexpected.

1. ALWAYS HAVE A PLAN B.

If you have a Plan B, it won't be as disappointing when your Plan A doesn't work. As I travel around doing seminars and training, I have learned to have even a Plan C or Plan D. I have my presentations on a flash drive as well as saved to the computer I am using. When I take my big projector, I take my small projector as a backup in case the big projector's bulb goes out. I carry a printed copy of my PowerPoint in case I have a total power outage. Having a Plan B can dull the pain of an unexpected disappointment. I was glad I didn't stop looking for work when my friend first told me about the position in her company. I had a Plan B that came through for me.

2. MONITOR YOUR EMOTIONS.

Keeping your emotions in check is critical. If not, the unexpected can have you say or do something you will later be sorry for.

When I was told the college position I had held for 5 years would be dropped and merged with another campus where the instructors had been there for a much longer time, I was devastated. I wanted to say, "Why did you bring me all the way up to Iowa from Florida, just to later say sorry, your job is no longer available?" I then had to continue to teach my classes and fulfill obligations for several more months. This was one of the most difficult times of my life. But I took the high road and held my head up and continued to do an excellent job for the rest of my contract.

3. PULL FROM YOUR INNER STRENGTH.

When the unexpected happens, pull from within. I have found the best thing I can do is to pray. I pray for God to help me through disappointments, humiliations, and trials. I have found when I ask for strength--I receive it. I also find it helps me to do something to take the spotlight off me and my problems. The best way to do that is to assist someone else.

When I have taught Psychology and Human Relations courses on the college level, I discussed how each person's resiliency is different and how each has a difference in their Locus of Control. I would often give students a short test to help them assess if their Locus of Control came from external sources or from internal sources. People with a high internal Locus of Control may sometimes blame themselves when things happen and say, "I should have seen it coming; it's all my fault." Those people need to understand sometimes things are beyond their control. However, they are also the individuals who can find the strength from within to keep on going when others give up.

We should all work on becoming more resilient. We're always going to have problems and find ourselves in unexpected situations. The more resilient we are, the better the chance we can get through what we have to go through to get to where we need to be.

I was always looking outside myself for strength and confidence, but it comes from within. It is there all the time. ~~~Anna Freud

4. FOCUS ON TOMORROW--NOT TODAY OR YESTERDAY.

A Beatles song says 'all our troubles seem so far away yesterday, and we should believe and long for yesterday." I think we all know we can't change the past. We may not even be able to handle what is happening today. But there's always hope for tomorrow.

I remember me and Mama discussing how Scarlett O'Hara in *Gone with the* Wind had said, "After all, tomorrow is another day." Scarlett said this after the love of her life had told her he didn't care what happened to her and then left her. Scarlet was a survivor. She had learned when things were too hard to handle today, we had to have hope and believe tomorrow would be better.

My favorite movie *Shawshank Redemption* also focused on how we should never give up hope no matter what we're going through. Andy tells his friend Red how "hope is a good thing and maybe the best of things." So focus on what you can do-- not what you didn't do or can't do.

* * *

WHAT I CAN DO TO ANTICIPATE THE UNEXPECTED.

If I were hanged on the highest hill,
Mother o' mine, O mother o' mine!
I know whose love would follow me still,
Mother o' mine, O mother o' mine!
If I were drowned in the deepest sea,
Mother o' mine, O mother o' mine!
I know whose tears would come down to me,
Mother o' mine, O mother o' mine!
If I were damned of body and soul,
I know whose prayers would make me whole,
Mother o' mine, O mother o' mine!
~~~Rudyard Kipling

CHAPTER SIX – REGARDLESS OF WHAT YOU BELIEVE, I'M FROM VINA.
(Know Who You Are and What You Stand For)

Mama loved Vina. She was proud to be from Vina, Alabama.

The "i" in Vina is a strong "i" pronounced like the "i" in kind or find. I often tell folks I grew up in a town so small it said "Welcome to Vina" on both sides of the city limits sign. I might tell that joke about Vina, but I love my hometown.

Mama retained a bit of her northern accent having spent her first 17 years in Wisconsin. When she met someone for the first time, they often would ask, "Where you from?" She always smiled and politely replied, "I'm from Vina." They would then say, "No I mean where you REALLY from?" She would lose a little of her smile and politeness and firmly reply, "As I said--I'm from Vina."

Mama taught me it was important to know who I was and what I stood for. It didn't matter to her where she came from; it only mattered where she was now.

I competed in saxophone and speaking competitions during my middle and high school years throughout Alabama. When I would win or place in those contests, my name and school would be called out or listed. The other winners were from large, well-known schools and would make fun of the name Vina or pretend they misheard the name. I stood up for myself and my town because of Mama's love for Vina and its people. I have had people try to make fun of my hometown and where I came from even today. In true "Mama" style, I always let them know I'm proud of who I am--especially concerning my Vina roots. I was a little upset at a recent survey a friend shared with me listing the 10 worst towns of Alabama in which to live. Vina was in the #1 position. That might be the author or researcher's opinion--it's not mine.

Mama Enjoyed This Vina House For More Than 40 Years. My Brother John Barker Still Lives Here.

The Vina school system granted me an excellent education--especially in the math and science areas. (Thank you Tommy Williams and Tommy Holcomb.) I decided to be a business teacher because of my business teacher Ms. Lucretia Alexander. She was beautiful, well spoken, and made her classes fun and interesting. My favorite business class was "Shorthand." I enjoyed learning and using a language most individuals can't read or understand. I still use the skill to take notes and keep some of my writings private. My elementary teacher Pauline Davis and middle school teacher Ruby Ray taught me moral values which guide me even to this day. These teachers not only taught those values, they epitomized them.

I remember the joy in Mama's voice and on her face the day she announced, "I guess that means I really am a Barker now." We had gone back to Wisconsin for her brother Leon's funeral. We stayed for part of the time with my cousin Jim Barker, whom we called "Dood." When a Barker relative found out we had stayed with Dood, she said, "Well, I sure am glad you had some of your family up there to help you through your sorrow." Dood and Mama were not related by blood. She had relatives in Wisconsin who were her "blood" kin. Yet the Barker relative, whether she knew it or not, had granted Mama a validation she had sought for years.

> **This above all; to thine own self be true,**
> **And it must follow, as the day the night,**
> **Thou canst not then be false to any man.**
> **Farewell, my blessing season this in thee.**
> **~~~William Shakespeare**

Polonius, in the Shakespearian play Hamlet, compels his son to be true to himself. Polonius wanted his son to be loyal to his own interests first. I think he wanted his son to realize before you can help others, you have to be able to feel good about yourself.

Dr. Phil McGraw discussed in his book *Relationship Rescue* how when you try to improve your relationships with others the first lifeline to throw out should be to yourself. He also stressed to be the best of who you are.

Always be proud of who you are, what you stand for, and where you came from. Why? Because my Mama said so.

Grandma Furman, Me, Daddy, Ronald and Mama In Front Of Our Vina House Shortly After Moving In.

* * *

WHAT I CAN DO TO KNOW WHO I AM AND WHAT I STAND FOR.

_____

_____

_____

_____

_____

She put off buying a new car or a new dress for herself so that I could have a better life. She poured everything she had into me.

~~~Statement by President Barack Obama about his Grandmother who was instrumental in raising him.

CHAPTER SEVEN – YOU GOT SOME FUZZ IN THERE AMONGST ALL THAT OTHER FUZZ. (Help Others)

Mama went to a Northwest Jr. College basketball game while I was head cheerleader. It was her first and only Northwest basketball game she attended.

During the halftime break, I went over to sit with Mama and was mortified when she pointed to a girl with a huge afro hairdo sitting a couple of bleachers below us. The girl had some white fuzz caught in her hair. Mama wanted to let her know about it.

I said, "No, Mama. Don't tell her." But Mama climbed down the two rows of bleachers and to my dismay blurted out, "Hey there. You got some fuzz in there amongst all that other fuzz." She then put her hand in the girl's afro and pulled out the white fuzz to show to her.

I was embarrassed until I heard the girl say, "Thank you so much. I appreciate your letting me know instead of allowing me to continue to go around with it in my hair."

I learned a valuable lesson. I learned we should want to help people and not allow them to wander around needing help and not receiving it. Mama may not have used the proper words to help the young girl, but she had the right intentions. You never know when you may have the chance to make a difference in the life of someone else.

I once received an email with a forwarded story about a nurse who escorted a tired, worried Marine to the bedside of his dying father.

The father was on strong medicine and could barely make out the image of his son standing by his bed. He reached out his hand, and the young Marine squeezed the father's hand to show he was there for him.

The nurse brought a chair so the Marine could sit beside his father. The Marine continued to sit with the older man throughout the night without letting go of his hand.

Each time the nurse suggested the Marine should take a break, he declined. The nurse often heard the Marine offering words of encouragement and love to his father.

At dawn, the old man died, and the Marine released the man's lifeless hand he had held all night. When the nurse started to offer sympathy, the Marine interrupted her by asking, "What was his name?" The shocked nurse replied, "He was your father." The Marine in a quiet voice said, "No. He wasn't. I had never met him."

"Then why, said the nurse, didn't you say something when I first brought you to him?" The Marine replied, "I knew right away there was a mistake, but I also knew he needed a son who was not here. He needed me, so I stayed."

The next time someone needs you--be willing to stay and help them.

I hope the following information will encourage you to help others:

1. LOOK FOR EXAMPLES.

Even though the media is filled with examples and innuendoes of people who hurt others, there are numerous examples of people who help. It all depends on what or whom you focus on.

A story I often tell my students when encouraging them to be positive intead of negative goes like this. The humingbird searches for beautiful red flowers to drink nectar from in the desert and the vulture searches the desert for rotten and dead carcasses to consume.

They both find what they search for. The humingbird searched for and found a cactus with flowers the hot sun kept alive. The vulture looked for and found the carcass of an animal the hot sun killed through dehydration and turned into rotten flesh. I then tell them to be careful what they look for in life, because that's what they will find.

I was in Port St. Lucie, Florida, reaching for the remote to turn off the TV before leaving my hotel room to give a seminar. A news story got my attention. It was about a 13-year-old Kentucky girl who helped a young boy she saw being bullied. The boy had shown up in her neighborhood to play basketball with some of the children. No one knew him, and soon he was bullied because of the old, torn up shoes he wore. The girl went inside her home and came out with a pair of sneakers to give him. Her mother posted an online video of what her daughter did, and it soon became a news story shown all around the United States.

The next day I saw how the news story had expanded to other children doing nice things for kids in their neighborhoods. One girl bought a new net for the basketball goal of a neighbor whose netting needed to be replaced.

2. LOOK FOR PEOPLE WHO NEED HELP.

Open your eyes and look around for someone who needs your help. Look for ways to be useful. It doesn't have to be a monumental sacrifice on your part. It can be a small thing.

I fly several times each month to provide training and seminars. When it's time to get off the plane and I'm in an outside seat, I stand up, back up, and leave space in front of me to let everyone in my row get out before I do.

I also ask everyone around me if I can get their overhead luggage down for them. These are small things I can easily do for others that do not cost anything and make me feel useful and helpful. Sometimes I believe it can help with jet lag. (Just kidding.)

3. BE APPROACHABLE.

We can miss a lot of opportunities to help others by marching through our lives without noticing other people.

By not making eye contact or refusing to smile or speak to those we have chance encounters with, we may lose on opportunity to be helpful.

I said hello to an elderly gentleman who sat next to me on a flight from Denver to San Francisco before I sat down beside him.

Later he showed me a brochure and asked me what a certain paragraph meant. He was from Seoul, Korea, visiting in the United States and had been to the Rocky Mountain National Park. The brochure had some United States colloquialisms in it he didn't understand. I was able to expain them to him, and he was most appreciative.

If I had not been approachable, he would not have asked for my help--nor would I have had the privilege to have helped him.

4. WHEN YOU HELP OTHERS, YOU HELP YOURSELF.

When you are making the decision to help someone, you are in control. It feels good to be in control. It does not feel good to be out of control or to be controlled.

Also, you are choosing to bring positive energy into your life. People who help others are happier and less depressed. Don't you believe this? A University of Massachusets medical survey said so.

Jesus used a parable to educate a crowd to show how they would reap what they sowed, and Apostle Paul told the Galatians not to be deceived because they would reap what they sowed. Most people when evaluating Jesus and Paul's teachings would use the principle negatively to announce, "You'd better stay out of trouble because you're going to reap what you sow."

I prefer to look at the positive side. If we do good, we will reap goodness. This is an exciting concept once you finally get it--especially if you want positive blessings to come your way.

Danielle Steel wrote a book entitled, *Blue,* where on a cold December night in New York City, the main character Ginny Carter had given up on life and was contemplating suicide. She saw a homeless boy named Blue sleeping in a shed and instead of her commiting suicide, she began concentrating on how to help him.

By helping him, she gained purpose to her life. It is so easy to end up bettering yourself when you start out to make someone else's life better.

5. JUST DO IT.

I recently read that 20% of people identify themselves as a chronic procrastinator. What about you? Are you a procrastinator? Are you approaching the chronic level?

Procrastinators tend to look for distractions to keep them from doing what they need to do. Stop looking for those distractions! Reach out and help when you can.

Some people don't consider themselves as being a procrastinator. They believe the time is not right. When the time is right, they will become more helpful. Unfortunately, many opportunities are lost never again to return.

If we're not going to do anything to help others, what is our purpose in life?

I heard the lyrics of a song asking basically why God let people hurt and suffer and why didn't he do something about it? At the end of the song the singer said that God did do something. He made you and me. He made me and you to do something to help others.

Phil Knight didn't just come up with the slogan "Just Do It" for his company . . . He "did" something.

This Co-Founder and Chairman of Nike, along with his wife Penny, agreed to donate $500,000,000 to OHSU (Oregon Health and Science University) if they would raise enough money to match it. It took the University 22 months to accomplish the feat.

It is incumbent on every one of us to do what he or she can do to keep the miracles coming. ~~~Phil Knight

OHSU now has $1 billion for cancer research. This money will help to detect lethal types of cancer. The plans are to recruit around 300 scientists to get the job done. If you want to contribute to the research, you can log into their website: onedown.org. Don't put off doing something to help others. Follow Mama and Phil Knight's example and . . .

JUST DO IT!

* * *

WHAT I CAN DO TO HELP OTHERS.

Tsekung, who was the most devoted Confucius disciple and first-class diplomat, was known to criticize. Confucius told him, "You may think you are clever, but I am more clever than you because I don't make time for such things."

Confucius also said, "Don't criticize other people's faults, criticize your own."

CHAPTER EIGHT – I'LL SEE YOU WHEN I SEE YOU. (Accept and Love Family Unconditionally)

Mama was always glad to see me no matter how little I came home, or how long I visited. She was never too busy to give me attention.

When I promised to visit and did not follow through with my intention, she would only say, "Well darling; I will see you when I see you."

If I left earlier than promised, I heard the same, "Well, darling; I will see you when I see you." Her love wasn't based on how often I visited or how long I stayed. She was always glad to see me and enjoyed every minute I visited or talked to her.

This is my favorite of Mama's sayings. When she said it to me, I knew it meant she loved me unconditionally. That love wasn't based on my accomplishments or lack of accomplishments.

The easiest way I can explain how she loved me unconditionally is to share what the Bible says love is. Mama loved me in all the ways listed on the next page.

LOVE
Is Patient
Is Kind
Does Not Boast
Is Not Proud
Is Not Self-Seeking
Is Not Easily Angered
Keeps No Record of Wrongs
Does Not Delight in Evil
Rejoices with the Truth
Always Protects
Always Trusts
Always Hopes
Always Perseveres
Never Fails.
~~~The Bible

Mothers are known to love their children unconditionally, but there are other examples of unconditional love in families.

Ma'ake Kemoeatu was a starter on the Baltimore Ravens team that won the Super Bowl. He fought hard to earn that starting position after being out a year with an injury. At the peak of his career, he gave it all up to donate a kidney to his brother Chris.

Because of his unconditional love, he made the statement, "If any of my siblings needed a kidney, it would have to be my kidney." The doctor conducting the transplant said Ma'ake's kidney was 1 and 1/2 times bigger than any kidney he had ever seen. Not only did he donate a kidney to his brother--it was a large, healthy one.

* * *

WHAT I CAN DO TO ACCEPT AND LOVE FAMILY UNCONDITIONALLY.

_____

_____

_____

_____

_____

CHAPTER NINE – DO YOU WANT TO TALK TO YOUR DADDY? (Show Respect)

I moved to Tuscaloosa a few days after my 19th birthday. Throughout my college years at the University of Alabama, I made sure I called home at least once a week. I continued this tradition throughout my professional and personal life until both my parents passed away.

Mama always answered the phone, with her signature, "Hey-low." Before we hung up, she would always ask, "Do you want to talk to Your Daddy?"

Respect for one's parents is the highest duty of civil life. ~~~Chinese Proverb

Mama showed proper respect to the father of her children. She wanted me to know I should also speak to Daddy.

I didn't have a lot to say to Daddy nor did he to me. I would ask, "How are your dogs doing?" He would say, "Fine." I would reply, "Have they won any more trophies?" He would say, "Yes--a few more." There would be silence. I would tell him I loved him, and I needed to go. He would ask, "When you coming home?" I would say, "Soon." Then he would say, "Bye." I would say, "Bye." Then we'd hang up.

I speak to everyone in the same way, whether he is the garbage man or the president of the university. ~ ~ ~Albert Einstein

Alfred Adler is my favorite person in the Psychology field. He believed our greatest fundamental desire is to belong and feel significant. He wrote when we experience respect, it helps us to feel fulfilled. Once we feel fulfilled, we are emotionally healthy.

Here are some ideas to show proper respect and become emotionally healthy.

1. DON'T IGNORE.

Do you enjoy being ignored? I don't. Neither does anyone else. We may occasionally want to be alone, but we never want to be ignored. Mama knew it was necessary for Daddy's presence in the room to be honored. She did not want him to feel ignored.

2. GIVE COMPLIMENTS AND BE GENEROUS WITH THEM.

Don't be afraid to praise someone who does a good job, whether it is on a personal or professional level. Every time I talked to Mama on the phone, she always said something nice about Daddy she thought I would appreciate. I enjoy giving other people compliments. If I like their hairdo, I tell them. If I believe that they are wearing a nice pair of shoes, I let them know. I don't have to know them or ever see them again.

3. ASK FOR AND RESPECT THE BOUNDARIES OF OTHERS.

My daughter Katie is a senior in college majoring in Human Resource Management while working on a Psychology minor. She recently shared with me some interesting points from an Addictions Psychology class she is taking. She said clear boundaries are essential, and healthy families have boundaries. Clear boundaries help an addictive personality to function better than if he/she is in a family with no limits. I noticed a page of her notes where she had written, "Boundaries are the rules of interactions and methods of functioning within families and society." Everyone should have boundaries, and we need to respect them. If you don't know a person's boundaries, you should ask. Once you know the boundaries, value them and follow them.

4. DO YOUR BEST TO KEEP YOUR PROMISES.

Follow through with what you promised you would do. Keeping your promise shows respect. It shows you think enough about the other person to keep your word. Giving your word means you have made a declaration that soon you will or will not do something specific. Maintaining a promise shows you value the other person.

5. DISCUSS WITHOUT ARGUING.

There's a difference between a discussion where two or more individuals express their different opinions and an argument. Lack of respect occurs when the discussion morphs into an argument. Especially when you expect me to honor your opinion without you honoring mine.

My Favorite Picture of Mama and Daddy.

* * *

WHAT I CAN DO TO SHOW RESPECT.

_____

_____

_____

_____

_____

My Aunts Maxine Barker and Idell Barker, Cousin Wilma Faye (Tootsie) Humphres, and Mama. I'm Sure They "Made Slaw."

CHAPTER TEN – LET'S MAKE SLAW.
(Nurture Relationships)

I hate to make slaw.

I hate peeling and chopping the despicable onion that makes my eyes water and occasionally even makes me sob.

I am terrified of the grater. It's an alien force focused on coming as close as it can to attack my knuckles. It often takes over my hands and mind to slings bits of cabbage and carrots all over my clothes, in my face, and up into my hair.

When Mama said, "Let's Make Slaw," I translated it to mean, "Judy--you make slaw because you need to be punished. I want you to be miserable doing something you hate to do."

After Mama passed away, I found myself thinking, *"I wish Mama was around to ask me to make slaw."*

Not that I was seeking punishment. (No I am not a masochist.) I realized when I came to Mama's kitchen and sat at the kitchen table "making slaw" was our alone time. She was usually taking the boiled potatoes out of the pressure cooker to add ingredients to and mash. Sometimes she washed a few dishes. She always asked me how I was doing and shared with me things she had been thinking about. Since everyone hated making slaw, my brother--later brothers, later husband, and later kids--gave us a lot of space. It was Mama/Judy time, and it was usually the only occasion we had private time. It was important for her to make sure we had this time to nurture our relationship.

The more a daughter knows the details of her mother's life, the stronger the daughter. ~~~Anita Diamant

She taught me how important it is to work on personal relationships even if it means doing things we might not want to do. Nurturing family relationships is so much better than arguing and complaining. Isn't it amazing the things we sometimes argue about?

Have you ever heard of Yuri Ticuic? He argued with his wife about how bad the food was she had recently cooked and stormed out of the house into a wooded area to become lost for over a month. He was finally found dehydrated and frostbitten. He survived by eating berries, leaves, and hay, which I'm sure were not even close to being as delicious as what his wife would have cooked for him. By the way, after he was found, he vowed never again to criticize his wife's cooking. Why do we have to have a crisis happen before we show proper respect to those we care about and to nurture our relationships?

What would you do if your cousin wore something for Easter dinner that you didn't like? Would you shoot her in the head with a handgun like someone did in Columbus, Ohio?

Ashton Kutcher has a twin brother with cerebral palsy. Ashton has always nurtured his relationship with his brother. Ashton began modeling to help pay for his brother's health and medical expenses, which lead to his acting career. If he hadn't cared about his brother and their relationship, he would not be the success he is today.

Is your Mama still living? If so, take Coach Bear Bryant's advice and call her. Take my advice and tell her you love her and how you can't wait to "Make Slaw." Mama will enjoy and appreciate your explanation of what those two words actually mean.

I want to sit at Mama's kitchen table just one more time to "Make Slaw." There's so much I haven't told her and she never got to tell me. I have way too many unanswered questions that only she has the answers to. I am saddened to comprehend I will never again "Make Slaw" with Mama. What I can do is be thankful for the times we did share. I can also have many "Let's Make Slaw" moments with my children which will continue to nurture our relationships.

* * *

WHAT I CAN DO TO NURTURE RELATIONSHIPS.

CHAPTER TEN – I'LL LIVE UNTIL I DIE. (Be Thankful)

In 1955, Frank Sinatra released the song, "I'm Gonna Live Till I Die," written by Mann Curtis, Al Hoffman, and Walter Kent. Frank crooned about how he would laugh instead of cry and not miss a thing.

Country music star, Clay Walker, wrote a song entitled "Live Until I Die" which was on his 1993 debut album. This song was inspired by his grandmother. He felt so strongly about the message he decided to use the title of the song as the title of the album. The song focuses on keeping the good values taught to you as a child, not worrying about the future, and living every day given to you.

Even though Frank and Clay's lyrics were tremendously inspirational, neither inspired or affected me the way the same words spoken by Mama did.

I experienced these words on May 29, 2007, and they are everlastingly burned into my brain. When she spoke them, she did so with a wry smile without a tear in her eyes, or a tremor in her voice, to an oncologist. Her actual words were, "Well then, I will live until I die." Then she turned to me and my cousin, Sandra, and said, "Where do you two want to go for lunch?"

There are so many reactions you could make when you are told you have terminal cancer. One of my beloved aunts, when she learned she had terminal bone cancer screamed so loud her husband, who was sitting outside the office in their car, heard her scream.

In this last stage of Mama's life, she never complained. She did not say, "Poor, pitiful me." She continued to live her life. Less than a month after Mama told the doctor she would live until she died, she passed away.

When a mother dies, a daughter's mourning never stops.

Mama was the most intelligent person I have ever known, and I have been around a lot of educated and smart people. She didn't have a college degree, but she was my Internet before there was the Internet. Today I can pick up my smartphone and say, "OK GOOGLE." I then hear a ping, ask a question, and usually receive the answer in a matter of seconds. When I used to call Mama and ask the answer to a question, she would immediately give me the correct answer, no matter the topic.

Even though Mama did not have the kind of life I would have liked for her to have had, she was thankful for every minute of it and lived every moment of it until she died.

We never know how long we will have with our loved ones. Let's not shut our eyes and miss the beauty of their smiles and love. We should find ways to be thankful and let our loved ones know how important they are to us. We should all take Mama's advice and "live until we die."

In the movie, *Shawshank Redemption*, Andy tells Red to get busy living or get busy dying. If we're not living our lives and being thankful for what we have, then we are already dead.

Incorporate the following steps daily to "live your life" and be more thankful.

1. LOOK FOR SOMETHING POSITIVE IN EVERY SITUATION.

It is often difficult to find a silver lining in those dark clouds around us. Yet there are countless examples of individuals when faced with unexpected trials and dark clouds, are able to find something positive that makes things better for them than what they initially hoped for.

David Cook planned to be a professional baseball pitcher but threw his arm out shortly before entering college. After this disappointment and negative experience, he turned his efforts to music. He went to the American Idol audition to support his younger brother Andy and was not prepared to try out for the title of American Idol.

David Cook did not become a college or professional baseball player, but he entered the American Idol competition, won the contest, and went on to have a successful musical career.

When you find a silver lining, it requires you to believe in yourself when no one else does. Around

1990, Jim Carrey drove his old Toyota up to Mulholland Drive in the Hollywood Hills. As he overlooked the city, he wrote himself a check for $10 million and dated it Thanksgiving of 1995. Jim was broke and disheartened with his inability to make it big as an actor and so wanted something positive to hang on to. It worked because when 1995 came around, he had starred in several blockbusters and was commanding $20 million for any motion picture in which he starred. Carrey buried that $10 million check with his dad as a tribute because his father had always supported his dream to become a star.

Ann Arnall in her divorce from her husband did not find anything positive in the almost $1 billion check she was offered. Her ex-husband, Harold Hamm, built Continental Oil from the ground up with her help. Since Ann was an economist holding executive positions in the company, she denied the amount and said she wanted and deserved more. She felt she deserved half of the $18 billion in stock and assets they had accumulated during their 26-year marriage. How much money does it take for us to find something positive in a bad situation? Later Ann did cash the check and took almost $20 million worth of property and retirement and banking accounts, saying she was going to continue to fight for more.

2. HAVE A "THANKFUL" JOURNAL.

Every day, write down at least a couple of things you are grateful for. They don't have to be dramatic. Examples could be, I am thankful to see my daughter's smile, I am thankful to be pain-free, or I am thankful to have a roof over my head. When you have a bad day or feel unthankful, pull out the Thankful Journal to read some of the things for which you are thankful.

Be thankful for what you have; you'll end up having more. If you concentrate on what you don't have, you will never, ever have enough. ~~~Oprah Winfrey

3. THANK THOSE WHO HAVE DONE SOMETHING GOOD FOR YOU.

When you thank someone, it can improve your mood. Enjoy the smile on the face of someone who is appreciated. Thank the person who holds your door open as you pass through. Thank the person who brings you that cup of coffee.

Thank as many people as you can every day in every way. It is hard to be depressed or unhappy when you look for people to be thankful to.

I often see service men and women in the airports and on my flights. I enjoy airline personnel and passengers acknowledging their sacrifices and thanking them for their service. If we fail to seize our moments of happiness and be thankful for them, they can drift away.

Below is a note of thanks, I put on Facebook after a dear friend of mine (Harold Gene "Tuck" Tucker) passed away who had been my friend for over 30 years. I only wish I had taken the time to thank him more when he was alive.

Thank you, Tuck, for being my friend and helping me get through some bad times. Thank you for being such a good friend to so many others as well. Thank you for your service to your country in the Vietnam War. Thank you for being such a good father to your son, Jeff. Thank you for being such a good son to your parents. Especially how you've helped your mother these past several years. I don't know what she's going to do without you. Thanks for being such a good brother, especially to your brother, Bobby, and taking care of his business and personal affairs after his passing. Most of all, Tuck, thank you for being you. Be sure to tell Bear Bryant up there in heaven I said hello. You WILL be missed. God bless you and your life. I love you. ~~~Your Friend, Judy B.

4. HELP SOMEONE WHO IS LESS FORTUNATE.

A young couple curiously watched an old man walking along the beach. He was gently placing starfish back into the ocean that washed ashore unable to get back into the water on their own. The young couple contemplated the large number of starfish littering the shore and knew the old man could not save them all.

They asked him why he did what he did since it really didn't make that much difference. As he placed yet one more of the starfish into the ocean, he said, "It made a difference to that one."

There are always individuals less fortunate than you. Look for them and do something for them without expecting anything in return. An individual who is less fortunate does not always mean he or she has less money or fewer material possessions than you. It could be someone who has fewer friends or does not have a loving spouse like you do.

5. SPEND QUALITY TIME WITH FAMILY AND FRIENDS.

One of the best ways to show your family and friends how thankful you are for them is to spend quality time with them. No matter how busy you are, block out time and be completely present. This means you should conquer those desires to do something like stare at your smartphone or text every few seconds.

A 2013 survey of 1,000 British parents indicated 95% of the parents felt the key to happiness was spending time with their family.

Quality time together with family was higher on the poll than material possessions, money, or career as a key to happiness.

Have scheduled family nights. They could consist of eating pizza and playing games, or watching a movie. This shows you are thankful for your family relationship and want to continue to cultivate it. When you spend quality time together, you can keep your family relationships strong. Relationships do not suddenly fall apart.

Several years ago a divorced friend of mine shared how her ex-husband suddenly ended their relationship with no warning. She said they had never had an argument, and she couldn't figure out why he asked for a divorce. I believe the relationship had to have started to deteriorate some time before, but she had been in denial.

A building doesn't suddenly fall to the ground, nor does a relationship suddenly fall apart. Years of abuse and neglect will cause that building to fall down. I saw a news story about Gary, Indiana, and how there were so many deteriorated buildings in their current condition because of the cold, harsh winters, and the wind off Lake Michigan. They deteriorated because no one spent any quality time with them.

When a hole appeared in the roof, no one repaired it, so the hole got bigger and bigger. Then rain and snow fell inside from the hole in the ceiling, and moisture damaged the floors and walls inside. Then there were more holes, more snow and rain, more moisture, and more and more damage to the floors and walls. I saw what had once been a beautiful church building totally fallen apart from neglect. Buildings and relationships must have upkeep, or they will erode over time.

Saturday, June 23, 2007, Mama peacefully passed away. As I held her hand, her breathing grew shallower and shallower until it completely stopped. She was surrounded by love. Her sons Ronald and John were in the room, as well as her nephew, Joe.

I often wonder why Mama had to go so soon. I miss her. I am constantly thinking, "Mama would enjoy seeing this or Mama would love this book." I still sometimes think, "Let me call Mama and tell her about this," only to realize I can't.

Have you ever questioned why God limits our days? The question was answered for me recently in the book *The Timekeeper*. Its author Mitch Albom in a narrative answers this question by saying it's because "each day is precious."

Here is a tribute my brother Ros wrote about Mama back in 2012.

This is mostly for my benefit, but I'd like to apologize to my mother. Mother, I apologize for: Not knowing what your dreams were . . . I'd bet washing dirty socks wasn't part of your dream. Expecting you to drop everything on a moment's notice because I had something I needed . . . Talking down to you . . . Telling you that "YOU JUST DON'T

UNDERSTAND" when it's now perfectly clear that you did understand and only wanted to prevent the pain that you knew would come . . . Taking advantage of your trust . . . Not loving you as much as you loved your four children . . . There is so much more I'd like to say, a hundred things, a thousand things. If Tam Barker were here today, even though it is after midnight as I'm writing this with tears in my eyes, I'd call her to tell her I love her. I do. The problem with that is I'm about five years too late. June 23, 2007, was my last chance to say, "I love you, Mom." I wish this were a Mitch Albom book, and I had you **FOR ONE MORE DAY**. ~~~Ros Barker, Jr.

Welles Crowther is a young man who exemplifies the concept of living until he died. He has been called *the man in the red bandana*.

Thursday, May 15, 2014, I was mesmerized as I watched the televised dedication of the National September 11 Memorial Museum located in New York City, New York. President Obama established this day as a national day of remembrance and service, and I heard him tell a very touching story about *the man in the red bandana*. Even more touching was when I saw Allison Crowther and Ling Young hold hands and heard them speak to the crowd and the cameras. Ling was one of the survivors of the 9/11 attack on the Twin Towers saved by *the man in the red bandana*.

Welles Crowther, a 24-year-old equities trader, was the man in the red bandana. Allison Crowther was his mother. Welles is credited with saving at least 12 people by helping them down from one of the Twin Towers to safety. He went back in multiple times to bring others out as he held his red bandana around his mouth and nose to keep out the smoke. When Ling Young met him, he was carrying a woman on his back. He then asked everyone to stand who could stand and anyone who could help to help. He had found an open stairwell and led Ling Young and several others down 17 flights of stairs (with the woman still on his back) to where others were there to help them down the remaining 10 flights to ground level.

Ling went down those last 10 flights to an ambulance to take her to a hospital, and the man in the red bandana went back up to help others. Within minutes, the building crashed to the ground.

Allison Crowther did not know Welles was a hero during his final moments until she saw a news story about how a lady named Judy Wein had been saved by a man in a red bandana. Allison knew it was her son because he always took a red bandana with him and had done so since he was a child to demonstrate a unique link to his father.

Even though Ling Young has had to endure 30 operations to repair what happened to her on September 11, 2001, she is thankful for what the man in the red bandana did for her. One of his red bandanas is on display at the National September 11 Memorial Museum, and Welles Crowther lives on in the lives of those he saved.

* * *

WHAT I CAN DO TO LIVE UNTIL I DIE.

_____

_____

_____

_____

_____

A mom's hug lasts long after she lets go. ~~~Author Unknown

PROLOGUE

The following words are part of the Eulogy given by my brother Ros at Mama's funeral.

" . . . We are gathered here today not to mourn the passing of a loved one but instead to celebrate a beautiful life.

Sunday morning I stood in the Red Bay Church of Christ's Fellowship Hall and listened to one person after another tell me how Tam Barker had affected their life. For those of you who don't know her let me summarize her life story and let you make your own decision as to who she was.

On May 7, 1936, Tamara May Furman was born to Helen Marie Navoiczyk Furman and Joseph Adam Furman of Kenosha, Wisconsin. Sixteen years later she graduated from Sacred Heart High school in Milwaukee, Wisconsin.

On July 3, 1953, she married my father after a five-week whirlwind romance and became the anchor point for the Barker Family.

My dad brought a young girl from Kenosha, Wisconsin, an industrial city just north of Chicago, to rural Franklin County, Alabama. She told me one time it was like going from the real world to the third world. I remember a story she told me about how my dad was going to teach her to drive and asked her where they could find a gravel road in Kenosha. In 1953, my mother had never seen an unpaved road.

She never quite lost her northern accent. Occasionally someone would ask, "Where are you from," and she would always reply, "Vina." They might press her further and eventually she would reveal she had been born in Kenosha, and the inquisitor would smile and say I knew you weren't from around here. To which she always replied, "I was born in Kenosha, but I have lived here since the 1950s. I've raised one daughter and three sons in Vina, regardless what you believe I'm from Vina!"

My mother came into a different world from the one she was raised in and never looked back. She never said, "You know I could have . . . " This was her home, and my dad's family became her family since her mother and brother were more than six hundred miles away.

Always a quick study, she was eager to learn about this culture which was so different from the one she had been raised in. She wanted to know all the family stories, and soon she became the archivist or keeper of the family records. Tam was the person to ask if you wanted to know when a family member was born, got married, or more somberly when they passed away. If there was a family event, Mother could tell you when it took place. Family members would ask my dad, and he'd say, "let me get back to you" and then came home and asked my Mom. Daddy might have been able to give you the year, but Mother could not only tell you what year it happened, but the exact date, what day of the week, and sometimes even what time of day.

If you needed help in filling out any type of paperwork, all you had to do was call mother. She might not know how to do it when you called, but by the time you arrived she knew. I honestly believe if you asked her how to fly a helicopter and told her you were bringing one over she would have the manuals by the time you arrived. She was everyone's sounding board. She said one time my dad was the poor man's lawyer. If you had legal problems, his years in law enforcement could help him help you make a decision, but if my dad was the poor man's lawyer, then my mother was the poor man's counselor and psychiatrist. If you had problems she would sit and listen, not passing judgment, knowing you didn't really need advice; you only wanted someone to listen. When you were finished talking she would reach over, pat your hand, and say something like, "Don't worry baby; it'll be all right." Or, "Give things a little time then see how you feel." I always knew who to go to with my problems, but never thought about who Mother went to with her problems.

As I sat to write this eulogy, I realized I knew exactly who mother confided her problems in. The Book of Matthew, Chapter 11, Verse 28, says: Come unto me, all ye that labor and are heavy laden, and I will give you rest. She was secure in her faith. She told me one time, "I would rather believe and live a Christian life to the best of my ability and find out later there is no God than to live my life believing in nothing and find out I was mistaken on the judgment day."

While making the arrangements for this service, Clarissa Deaton asked what my mother did, and the family answered Mother was a homemaker. But she was more than that.

She was a psychiatrist, doctor, nurse, counselor, archivist, teacher, researcher, spiritual leader, accountant, and role model. All good mothers are.

As I was looking through Mother's Bible, I found a poem named AFTERGLOW, my cousin, Rita Thrasher Brown, sent to Mother in 1980; the family felt it was appropriate to read it here today.

I'd like the memory of me
To be a happy one.
I'd like to leave an afterglow
Of smiles when life is done.

I'd like to leave an echo
Whispering softly down the ways
Of happy times and laughing times
And bright and sunny days.

I'd like the tears of those who grieve
To dry before the sun
Of happy memories that I leave
When my life is done.

My mother wasn't great in the sense that she set out to change the world, and did. Tam Barker changed the world in little-unseen ways. She changed her world through her faith.

To those of you who never had the privilege of meeting my mother, I extend my sympathies to you and say I am sorry for your loss.

***

In the end, it's not the years in your life that count, it's the life in your years.

~~~Abraham Lincoln

The following are some other things Mama said along with a short explanation that didn't make it into the major part of the book.

1. DON'T LET YOUR BROTHER CRY.

From the day Ronald came home from the hospital, I wanted to take care of him.

I remember one time in particular when Mama told me, "I have to go outside for a few minutes, and don't let your brother cry." Within seconds of Mama going outside, Ronald started crying. I told him very nicely to stop that crying because Mama said I wasn't to let him cry. He didn't stop so I spanked his legs. That made him scream at the top of his lungs.

When Mama came back in and asked what happened, I told her. I thought she would be proud of me punishing him because he had cried. Instead, she told me when Daddy got home, I would be getting a spanking--which I did.

I learned a valuable lesson that day. Just because you have power, you don't have to abuse it.

2. WELL HONEY--IF THAT'S WHAT YOU WANT.

I never remember Mama ever criticizing me. She allowed me to make the important decisions in my life without telling me I couldn't do something or needed to do something else. When she was a little doubtful of whether it was a right decision, she simply said, "Well honey--If that's what you want." I immediately knew I needed to rethink the matter or do some more research. I never felt dumb or stupid. Instead, I felt in control of my life and my destiny.

3. YOUR MAMA.

Every letter or card she ever wrote me was signed "**Your Mama**." She wanted me to know she was My Mama, and I could always depend on her. There was no doubt that she was proud of me and accepted me as being **Her Daughter**.

* * *

Other books by Judy Barker Austin

Always Take The High Road In Your Professional, Personal, And Financial Life

Available at:

https://www.createspace.com/5596239
or amazon.com

Excerpt:

What do you listen to as you travel The High Road? Local and national news on the radio? Motivational messages or favorite songs on CDs or MP3 Players? Do the things you listen to inspire you to be a better person and achieve your dreams? What are your dreams? Are they large enough for The High Road? How is your vision? Is it limited? Limited vision can limit dreams.

There was a frog at the bottom of a well. He looked up and thought the sky was only as big as the top of the well. The frog's dreams were small and he was unmotivated to do anything except to be unhappy and stay in the well because of his limited vision.

THE GOD COMPLEX--Family Secrets

Available at:

https://www.createspace.com/5682690
or amazon.com

Excerpt:

As Peter picked up Papa's Bible to return the prayer, an envelope fell to the floor. He retrieved it, tore it open, and found three unusual keys inside. As he turned the keys over and over in this hands, questions filled his head. *What are these keys for? Why hadn't Papa given them to me before now? What did Papa mean when he said there were family secrets?*

For the first time in his life he felt weak and helpless. He realized he was not ready to relinquish Papa's guidance, wisdom, and love.

In a room nearby, Papa's private duty nurse and housekeeper heard a bloodcurdling wail and ran into the bedroom to find Peter sobbing and tightly holding Papa's frail body.

Look for more High Road Books now in the works to help you stay on The High Road.

Schedule up-to-date training and seminars for your organization or business.

Contact: Judy Austin
P. O. Box 94
Centerville, IA 52544
judybarkeraustin.highroad@gmail.com

www.ingramcontent.com/pod-product-compliance
Lightning Source LLC
Chambersburg PA
CBHW070205100426
42743CB00013B/3050